In the Water

by Anne Giulieri
illustrated by Anna Hancock

The fish is in the water.

The frog  is in the water.

The duck is in the water.

The turtle is in the water.

The elephant is in the water.

The monkey is in the water.

The crocodile is in the water.